T0171612

Kundalini Quest

Warriors of light, wake up the time is at hand

Kim Boten

BALBOA.
PRESS
A DIVISION OF HAY HOUSE

Balboa Press books may be ordered through booksellers or by contacting:

Balboa Press
A Division of Hay House
1663 Liberty Drive
Bloomington, IN 47403
www.balboapress.com
1-(877) 407-4847

Because of the dynamic nature of the Internet, any web addresses or links contained in
this book may have changed since publication and may no longer be valid. The views
expressed in this work are solely those of the author and do not necessarily reflect the
views of the publisher, and the publisher hereby disclaims any responsibility for them.

The author of this book does not dispense medical advice or prescribe the use
of any technique as a form of treatment for physical, emotional, or medical
problems without the advice of a physician, either directly or indirectly. The
intent of the author is only to offer information of a general nature to help you
in your quest for emotional and spiritual well-being. In the event you use any
of the information in this book for yourself, which is your constitutional right,
the author and the publisher assume no responsibility for your actions.

Any people depicted in stock imagery provided by Thinkstock are models,
and such images are being used for illustrative purposes only.

Certain stock imagery © Thinkstock.

ISBN: 978-1-4525-5357-3 (sc)
ISBN: 978-1-4525-5356-6 (e)

Printed in the United States of America

Balboa Press rev. date: 8/16/2012

INTRODUCTION

"When the student is ready, the teacher shall appear"

When I was a kid making my way through life I never said "When I grow up I want to be a Light Worker" in fact until recent years I probably would have thought that meant you were some type of electrician. A lot has changed since then and I did grow up to become a "Warrior of the Light" we are the way showers. Awakening to help show the way, we are being divinely guided toward our true calling in life. This is a blessed and highly spiritual time we have been born into. We are the generation that is awakening to be the catalyst to change the old into the new.

Mother Earth is crying out, Father God is sending all Angels, Angels are guiding all Light Workers, all Light Workers are preparing to help guide the masses that are waking up. We as a people, every age religion, and nation are consciously realizing that we can no longer go on in separatism or as usual, nor should we even care to. The as usual seems unusual to me...

PROLOGUE

We are awakening. We truly are the generation that is witnessing the end of the old and the beginning of the new. As written by Jesus "As it is in Heaven so shall it will be on Earth" this is the meaning of "As above so below as below so above" 2012 ushers in a new way of thinking and feeling that only needs to be understood not feared. The point of this publication is for me to share my journey to better assist anyone having fear associated with 2012 and all the mystery that surrounds the date and time as a dooms day. When in actuality I believe it is the long awaited "Golden Age". This event will change the hearts and minds of all of humanity, ushering in the harmonics of peace and love. As Jesus said "We will not all sleep but will all be changed" I for one am welcoming this change.

I have spoken to so many people that are showing the signs of awakening and I find that in the beginning none want to hear what I have to say. Yet once the signs persist and the veil continues to lift they become ready to receive some answers and guidance. It's not easy at first; in fact it's confusing and surreal. We have been deceived for so long that it's become a way of living that humanity has grown to except. Once you wake up to the facts you will not turn back, you will steadfastly want to move forward on the quest for your own journey toward the light. It will become your insatiable need to seek the truth of who you really are and what your true purpose is. We are all amazing intelligent spiritual beings with a gift to share with the world. A new era is about to manifest on our planet. I have read about, studied, and hoped for this moment in time for many years.

I feel blessed to be alive and part of this change, the shift in consciousness so desperately needed for our world to continue to sustain us. I for one welcome it with great anticipation and excitement. It is my hope that in reading this book you will share the same conclusion.

CONTENTS

CHAPTER 1

WHAT JUST HAPPENED

One evening for no apparent reason I fell unconscious at the foot of my bed. I awakened to my partner, paramedics, and a friend. As the tunnel-type vision and foggy feeling subsided I assured everyone I was fine. I had been working long hours in a very high stress environment and assumed I was probably just in need of a long relaxing tropical vacation. Wrong, these episodes continued to happen. After countless Doctor visits' involving every test imaginable the results were in; I am an extremely healthy, sane human being, having a major spiritual experience. It was then that my quest truly began. Bringing me to this moment in time to share my experience, strength, and hope with others having similar experiences.

The ringing in my ears, the sound of harps, blurred vision, and muscle aches. I experienced extreme bursts of energy followed by exhaustion; I thought I was going insane. The fact is, I was finally waking up from a deep sleep, and once I realized this my whole world began to change. "The veil had been lifted" and I was able to see, my mind was literally flooded with the need for new knowledge. I spent numerous sleepless nights reading, listening, and learning about the true nature of the universe and who I am. This was only the beginning of a journey that has led me to here and now, to this exact moment in time. This is the true story of my awakening to the reality of our planet and my shift in consciousness. At first I had no idea what was going on. I soon discovered that the Kundalini dragon had risen in me and what that means.

I had an urge to delve deeper into the ancient history and origins of the Kundalini. This is the type of research I have always done on everything; where did it originate? What does it all mean, literally and symbolically as a people striving for answers in a seemingly uncertain time in our history? I discovered that it's truly an amazing time in human history to be alive. We are evolving from lower energy mind and body, into higher energy mind and light body. Our DNA is changing, time is speeding up, and our chakras are awakening from 7 to 12 causing us physical pain, as we evolve. Psychologist Carl Jung called the chakras the "gateways of consciousness". They are connected to our thinking and feeling through our breath, through our body, through our voice and through movement. When we are not aware of our chakras, they operate on a subconscious level.

If a person has no concept of anything beyond the material, the chakras are 'dormant'. When we start to question who we are, and what our purpose is, and begin to develop our divine nature, the chakras become active and our spiritual mind will start to develop. None of this is odd or shocking to me, as a youth I had sought out answers to so many of the questions that are now being revealed and made clear to me. For 12 years I had studied Revelations through commentaries along with the quatrains of Nostradamus, and several other prophets, teachings, and beliefs relating to what were termed the end time prophesies. I have always had a fascination with the Great Pyramids of Egypt, the Essenes, the lost spiritual art of Alchemy, UFO's, crop circles, the Hopi prophesy, and the Mayan calendar; I could go on and on. The point is all things seemingly mysterious always seemed to hold the key for me.

Somehow I have always known that something was wrong, people just weren't right. We didn't treat each other right; things have always seemed off to me. I was raised to be religious although I never resonated with that. I've always been spiritual and I bless all paths to God. I know now that we are the generation I studied about and hoped for all these years. What an amazing and exciting time it truly is to be alive. I am honored to be a part of the greatest change to ever happen in all of humanity. This shift in consciousness will literally change our way of thinking and life as we know it forever. We will know a new freedom and happiness that has long escaped us, it is our birthright to thrive and create a new reality together. All I can say is buckle your seat belts and get ready for the trip of your life.

The quickening torus of energy and frequency will continue to increase preparing our minds and bodies for the next stage of humanities conscious evolution.

CHAPTER 2

THE DRAGON HAS RISEN

I n my quest for the answers to what I was going through physically, I realized more and more as time passed that I was going through something much deeper than a medical issue. Everything kept coming back to Kundalini rising, meaning: "the awakened" power located in the first chakra at the base of the spine. The color representing this lower chakra is red. In ancient history this energy was depicted by a wingless serpent dragon, wingless represents the inability to rise to true enlightenment. This symbolizes the lower energy of ego-based thinking. The winged dragon represents the awakened and rising energies of enlightenment.

The awakening of this sleeping winged serpent dragon represents the upward spiral ascension of the masculine and feminine aspects of the spirit. The two becoming one through harmonic convergence. I had a pressing urge for more knowledge; I spent countless hours day and night reading, discovering new truths, and uncovering old lies. Lies I grew up believing to be the absolute truth. Beliefs passed down to me from my parents who were deceived. I started to experience a disconnection about who I always thought I was and what I always thought I believed. I became confused, exhausted, and depressed at times. Yet I had an inner knowing that I had to keep searching, researching, reading, uncovering and discovering the truth about who we are. As I passed through the feelings and mixed emotions of the deceptions, I would always find the truth.

It was as though I was being divinely guided. I know now I had been guided all along and that this was just the beginning of a long yet worthwhile journey. It became painfully clear to me painfully clear to me just how deep seeded we are with fear propaganda that has long served the few at the expense of many. Some fears were subtle while others were glaring, but still I became acutely aware of them and the feelings attached. The more I discovered the more I discarded and it began to lighten the heavy subconscious load of bullshit I had been dragging around for years. What a drag, in all seriousness though, what a waste of good energy. With a lighter load I became a better traveler, even though I had no idea where I was going; call it blind faith. Through all of this a phenomena kept happening 11:11 kept popping up, I mean really popping up.

The time of a certain email, a missed phone call, the time I went to bed, the time I made a call, it just went on and on. It was nothing new to me because I had an awareness of it through the years; I even did a little research on it in the past. The difference was now I was keenly aware of it and it was no longer a coincidence. I would ask for guidance every time it would happen. Sure enough as you'll hear me say again and again "when the student is ready the teacher shall appear" this just happened to be an inside job so no appearance was necessary. Although the intuitive guidance has been very clear to me, when all of this first started to happen I wasn't sure if it was my own thinking, insanity, or divine inspiration. Now I can easily differentiate between my heart, mind, and spirit. In the beginning I spent a lot of time just learning about what was going on with me physically, spiritually, and emotionally. It was in the seeking that I continually found the answers.

CHAPTER 3

11:11 THE WAKE UP CALL

The angels are calling; it's time to wake up from the stupor we have been in for eons. For me 11:11 became the next sign or should I say assignment to research until I truly understood its significance. As it turns out this phenomena's happening all over the world. 11:11 is a calling to those being awakened, called to action, to a deeper understanding of this numeric sequence and its significance to our evolution into higher consciousness. The sun having an 11.11 year cycle, and the winter solstice of 2012 falling at 11:11, people all over the world are finding themselves bombarded with 11:11. Just as science is predicting some kind of majestic solar event at the peak of this current cycle.

It's no mere coincidence; there is no doubt that the Sun has massive effects on Earth's biosphere. We sometimes forget that we do not merely orbit the sun but reside deep within its magnetosphere, the invisible part of the sun that generates a spherical torus enclosing our planet. The sun's rays transmit all the colors of the rainbow; each color holds a frequency needed for us to have a healthy mind and body. These rays enter through the retina of our eyes and travel through the brain synchronizing the right and left hemispheres. This energy continues down our spine and through the chakras of our bodies infusing us with essential energies. Many experts have contended that changes in the atmospheric ionosphere effects human and animal behavior, influencing biological, physiological, and behavioral patterns of all living things.

Certainly we know that some frequencies of radiation from the sun affect cell division and brain functions. Excess or lack of certain frequencies and types of solar radiation has been observed to have radical effects on human beings. The reason why the Sun becomes important in the 11:11 subject is not simply the solstice point in our calendar. It just so happens that the sun's magnetic field operates at a cycle of polarity reversals averaging 11.11 years in length. The next peak of this cycle happens to be in the year 2012 and has been predicted by some astrophysicists to most likely be a very active maximum. So as you can see when you do further research on the current events happening in and around our planet, it's getting easier and easier to read the writing on the wall and harder to stay in a state of denial.

In short 11:11 is another very significant piece of the puzzle I felt intuitively guided to put together. Beginning to answer the questions of who I am and who we are as one. I literally cried out in anguish to God to unveil my purpose to me. I needed more clarity, some sanity and sleep. As promised "Ask and you shall receive."

CHAPTER 4

THE VIEL HAS BEEN LIFTED

When I say I cried out to God I literally cried out in pain and anguish; I was so exhausted. Months had passed and I was still so uncertain about what this all meant and my role in the scheme of things. Instead of things calming down they became darker for me. I just couldn't find my center; I thought I was having some kind of nervous breakdown. I started feeling like my family couldn't take much more of my seemingly insane behavior. Yet, I intuitively knew I had to stay spiritually strong and focused on this journey. I have never been a weak hearted person.

While I was going through my internal unraveling of old belief systems, I was being restored with new truth. I had been working at the same company for almost four years, I loved my job and the people there; I missed them, they had become like family to me. I didn't even know how to express what I was going through without sounding as though I should be wearing paper shoes locked in a little padded cell. So I started avoiding many of the people I love during this part of my journey. I just did not know how to articulate what I was feeling or going through at this point. At home my family seemed to be looking at me as though I was from another planet. In fact, I started to feel like I was from another realm of existence. I was used to being the main provider in our home and I had no clue how that was going to play out.

Then sure enough I received an overnight envelope containing my former employee notice. At work we were like a team, a family, and I had already felt as though I was letting them down. Once I received that letter I felt my world as I knew it just falling apart around me. Yet I knew that all was exactly how it was supposed to be. It was such a deep inner knowing and certainty that it somehow kept me going. It was in the deep inner knowing that I found my next burst of inner strength. I received a blast so full of energy and pure white light that I couldn't breathe normal. It happened when I was falling asleep one night, I knew somehow that my life had changed forever. I was ready to embrace the change and flow with it instead of fighting, and trying to figure it all out.

I needed to take it easy and breath. It was then that I could hear a strong clear peaceful inner voice clearly and intuitively say, "The Veil Has Been Lifted"

CHAPTER 5

SLOW DOWN AND LISTEN

The message seemed clear enough to me although I found it to be harder than I imagined. I think for the first time in my life it became clear to me just how distracted people really are by a bunch of insignificant things. It's like the rabbit from Alice in Wonder Land and the mad hatter. I truly had to learn how to slow down and listen. To slow down mentally, emotionally, and physically is a much taller order than I imagined. This is when the journey into brain synchronizing and meditation began for me. I had to learn how to meditate and quiet my mind enough to hear my inner voice.

I really needed to understand and practice meditation on a deeper level. Eventually everyone in our home did some type of meditation. I started to notice the positive effect all this was having on us as a family. We were all more tolerant of the things that use to annoy us about each other. We hardly watched TV anymore, we started to exercise together, and read together; it was a nice change we were genuinely much happier. Now we all have our own individual style and type of meditation that we like. My partner and I listen to all types of meditation. Our son loves the brain sync that athletes do before a big game. Our daughter loves meditation with sounds of nature and music. Needless to say things had calmed down and our home showed the affect the meditation had on all of us.

It was about this time in this quest for truth that the next surge of energy and urge to learn about energy and chakras happened. I will go deeper into this in the chapter on "Tuning the Frequencies" At this point in my journey, I was still trying to make sense of it all. The only thing I knew for sure was not to stop, question, or give up. I haven't and I won't. It was then that I crossed paths with a woman that works with the chakras. I'm sure now I was destined to meet her. She came to our home and did some work with my energy to help ground my crazy, exhausted, over energized ass. She said to me, "You have a very strong calling and purpose but you already know that don't you?" Somehow I did know, I just didn't know exactly what I was being called to do yet.

I sure was doing a lot of research and retraining of every preconceived notion I had about life. It was as though I was being rewired with the truth and awareness of who we really are and how deeply connected we are to each other, our Creator, and Mother Earth in all her wonder and beauty. I needed a much deeper understanding of polarity and balance. I was about to embark on the next phase of my quest.

CHAPTER 6

JOURNEY INTO THE DARK

I kept myself grounded and started to meditate longer and more often. This was very beneficial and calming for me, now that my sanity had returned and I had truly slowed down enough to listen. I began to receive a whole new level of awareness and guidance. It was becoming much easier to hear what I needed to hear, go where I needed to go, and learn what I was guided to learn. It was very important to be grounded at this point of my awakening. What I was shown next was so dark and disturbing at times I had trouble mentally and spiritually processing all of the dark energy.

Now as I look back I can see why I needed to learn more about how to stay spiritually fit. I will be sharing some of the things that really helped me in the chapter on "Tuning the Frequencies". So the big questions kept coming up, why am I here? Who am I? What's my purpose? I was about to find out. During my research into energy generated by the great pyramids and sacred geometry it became clearer and clearer to me that something had went terribly wrong back then. So I was prompted intuitively to delve deeper to discover the answers. As I have learned, the answer is in the asking. And so I was shown one ugly truth after another. The deceptions began centuries ago and have been diabolically maintained since then until this present moment in time. We are awakening at this present time to turn things around before humanity ends up destroying itself and mother earth in the process.

I could write a whole book on the dirty dark secrets of the few that rule the many. Specifically Illuminati also known as the dark cabal, among others, these are the dark energies at work, the Hitler's of humanity. I don't want to give much energy to this as I have already been down this dark disturbing road and don't care to revisit it. In short Masonic conspiracies, murders, and world manipulation have been going on for eons. Below I shared keywords that cover some of the plans the dark cabal had for humanity. I also want to assure you that God, all the Angels in Heaven and the Galactic Federation of Light are with us and we will prevail. In fact many thousands of arrests are going to take place to free us from the tyranny. Still I am going to provide you with some key words for some online research. This way when you can't take any more you can simply stop.

Remember, half the battle is knowledge, the other half is waking up to the facts. This is a spiritual war so live from the heart, anger and rage feed the beast; love will destroy it once and for all. That is how we will end this war of terror and fear that's been waged against all of humanity and the earth that sustains us.

KEYWORDS & PHRASES

HAARP, Chemtrails, Depopulation, FEMA death camps, FEMA coffins, New World Order, Project Blue beam, Murals at Colorado Airport, RFID chips, Georgia Guide stones. Not a very enlightened bunch, as you'll soon see.

I recommend you at least do enough research to realize the importance of strong movements and messages for change, like Occupy Wall Street, The Shift Movement, World Alliance, New World Charter, Unify Earth, The Shift Network, and so many other amazing groups and individuals are rising up. God has heard our prayers, it is done and we are shifting and awakening. We are many, enlightened and strong. The Ascended Masters, the Hierarchy of Heaven, and the Federation of light have all been assisting in our ascension and evolution process.

CHAPTER 7

JOURNEY INTO THE LIGHT

After the last chapter I needed to embark on an even deeper journey into the light. I gave you some keywords and phrases. If you did any research at all then you basically already know where I've been, emotionally and spiritually. To gain an in depth understanding of the dark side I studied deeply the power associated with the alignment of pyramids. I also study Alchemy and its importance for our connection to source. Ancient numeric codes, Hermeticism, sacred geometry, 2012 and Mayan Scribes. The tragic deception against the Essenes. The massacre and genocide of whole tribes and Nations throughout history.

The Suppression of clean technologies specifically Nicola Tesla's free energy technology. I could go on and on, but the point of all of this studying, reading, and unraveling of one deception after another since the dawning of time, was exactly what I needed to take my 11:11 call to awaken seriously. The veil truly had been lifted and I answered the wakeup call. Now I needed some serious grounding after months of this type of learning. I truly was depressed and spiritually and emotionally exhausted. The phrase "burden of proof" never made so much sense to me as it did at this juncture in my quest. The common denominator in all of this is; any good thing or cause throughout history had been deceitfully taken out of the light and used for the dark. Used by any means for sheer power, greed, and control no matter how many had to die on the way. So in my low I was given a strong new high.

This is when I started to really understand the contrast of dark and light. The dark I am aware of in others or have experienced in my life is in contrast how much polar opposite I can experience, and hold in me with a strong intention for change and love towards others. The positive and negative polarities of life, have helped me in understanding the dark so I can shed more Light. The more I know the more I grow and strengthen myself for the task at hand. This is how we expand in consciousness. Now I am better equipped with my awareness; by knowing the dark so to speak, rather than being in denial, or acting as if everything is fine when it clearly is not. This is when I crossed over into the light with deeper purpose and inner knowing. I was now in a sort of flow of existence; I wasn't questioning life as often, I was just showing up for it moment by moment.

I let go of my baggage from the past and was no longer worried about the future. I was much lighter, patient, and easy going. I lost my need to control and be right and allowed people to be who they are without judgment. It was as though I saw the world with different eyes; the eyes of my spirit. I felt the world with thoughts of my heart, not my mind. I had changed profoundly and I felt different. I felt truly alive for the first time in years. I didn't realize how out of touch I was, how disconnected we all are from each other until I had truly awakened. I began to learn more about the connection I was having with intuition. This is when I started to receive a clearer channel with less static. I am definitely being guided by a higher source than my own thinking that's for sure. I use to go right when I felt I should go left, I am stubborn by nature and I know I've been a hard nut to crack.

Still I can honestly say my inner voice is strong and I do hear and listen now. We all have guardian Angels and guides, we always have, quiet yourself and pay attention. I now know I am being guided by Voloque the collective consciousness of 11 White Winged Angels of the ninth dimension. My dear friend Jeri used to always say to me, "Don't be so earthly good that you're no heavenly good, or so heavenly good that you're no earthly good" I really get that on a gut level now. Humanity is waking up from a deep sleep, we are changing rapidly, our DNA is changing, time is speeding up and our planet is tired. We have tons of work to do; I have been rewired, retrained, and reconnected with millions of other people on our planet having the same experience.

I am A Warrior of Light here to help guide those that are divinely led to me, as I am divinely led to those I need to accomplish my calling. Together we will forge a new future for our planet. 2012 marks the end of old infrastructures and behaviors that no longer serve us or our planet. 2012 ushers in a new beginning with sustainable energies, technologies, and thinking needed to heal ourselves and our planet. We are all taking this journey; are you prepared? If you are reading this, it's no mistake. We will all get what we need when we need it. I have always admired the phrase, "When the student is ready the teacher shall appear" I am no guru or saint I am you and you are me; we are all one. We have to get that! We are not separate, by color, sexual identity, beliefs, job titles, what you do or do not have.

Separate we are weak, together we are a mighty force; separatism is how we have been controlled for centuries, it's time for unity and synergy.

CHAPTER 8

VOCATIONAL TRANSITION

Next I was led through a vocational transition it was like being in a spiritual boot camp. I was flooded with new and unexpected knowledge. I felt like our home had turned into a University with all the books, binders, homework, and online classes. Webinars, seminars, and documentaries; wow I'm getting exhausted just writing this. I studied day and night. I learned the most amazing and beneficial things, my life changed forever. I have been coaching and counseling people for years but now I have so much more to give. Once again, it's in the asking that we do receive.

I am a Certified Life Coach I also studied as an Ambassador for Peace and actually received an invitation to the UN Peace Summit in New York. I just finished a great course on Conscious Evolution. By now I'm sure you can see I love to learn and I love knowledge. That's why I have always loved the saying "When the student is ready the teacher shall appear." Vocational transitioning will be different for everyone and not necessary for all. One thing I have found regarding the awakening is that part of the process involves a vocational transition. For most individuals to live your true life purpose you'll have to allow your divine guidance to assist you with your hearts true desire. Yet as always with all things we always have the free will to choose. I can only speak for myself here, when I say it's in the allowing that the divine works through me as a vehicle.

I carry out whatever task or message I am guided to deliver to whomever and wherever I am called to deliver. I will always end up exactly where I should be if I am in the present moment and paying attention to the inner intuition, my guiding voice. You know when you strongly feel like you should say no, but you say yes and regret it later. Or you are thinking of a good friend you haven't seen in years and you get a phone call a few minutes later. This is telepathy, your inner most guidance, or whatever you call it for you. We are all capable of connecting with this innate power of the universe, the power given us by our loving Creator. Remember, the answer is in the asking. My Grandparents raised me part of my life. I remember my Grandfather telling me when he was 83 years old that he was still learning something new every day.

So age is never an obstacle or factor when you feel a strong call to anything worthwhile. At this juncture of my journey I realized I was becoming hyper sensitive to sound and people's vibes, especially when they were strong negative or angry vibes.

CHAPTER 9

TUNING THE FREQUENCIES

L ike the beautiful orchestration of music tuned to the perfect frequency or your car when the engine's tuned just right and the fluids are all topped off. Our bodies also need to stay tuned to the right frequencies to experience optimal health and energy. This is an area I have always found to be crucial to my wellbeing. Biochemically our bodies cannot live without water or salt. Our blood needs holistic salt, I'm not talking about table salt; table salt poisons our body. The link below has high quality holistic salt; they also have an amazing book I highly recommend called **"Water & Salt"**

Kim Boten

http://www.himalayancrystalsalt.com

Our bodies also need the nutrients in raw organic fruits, nuts, and vegetables. This is essential for optimal health and energy. Organic food needs to be understood to be appreciated, especially in contrast to genetically modified food. Really the bottom line is the vitamins and nutrients from the sun and the minerals from the ground are what our bodies need, period. The sun and earth's energy is infused into organic fruits, nuts, and vegetables. That really is the simple truth; if it's not grown the way it was intended to be since the dawning of time then guess what? Something just isn't right. When you walk into most produce sections of a grocery store lined with pretty, colorful fruits and vegetables they are not what they appear to be. They do not have anywhere close to what our bodies need to function the way we should.

In fact any bit of good they may possess is diminished by all the poisons you ingest from the pesticides alone and the diseases associated with those poisons. I'm not writing this to convince or convert anyone. I am sharing my story to assist as many people as I possibly can who are having similar experiences. We need healthy, energy producing, live foods. The fact is we are changing and with this change you may eventually have to face the facts about what you eat. Or continue to suffer the consequences of eating heavy over cooked nutritionally dead foods. When I went through this part of my journey it was hard at first, I come from a steak and potatoes family. As time passed I slowly had to change what I could or could not eat. It got to the point that if I chose to eat it anyway I would feel bloated, sick and tired; I just wanted to feel healthier. Well I can honestly say I feel great now and full of energy.

I hardly need any food at all to fuel my body so to speak. Three big meals a day was just a way of life I lived for so many years. Although I'm the only one in our home that eats almost all raw foods, it's important for some of us on this journey to completely change the way we eat or suffer the consequences, you'll know intuitively. For me I try to get a daily dose of sun, water, raw honey, nuts, holistic salt, and live organic fruit and vegetables. It's a big part of my spiritual awakening. As a result I have tons of energy, my mind and body have quickened, and my frequency stays pretty high. I am not suggesting this for everyone; this is my true experience, thus far on this journey food has played a big part of my awakening. A plant based diet has become the cornerstone of my spiritual growth, healing and energy level. Sun plays a major role here, as mentioned earlier yet worth repeating.

Just 10 minutes of the sun's rays emanate the seven colors of the rainbow, the same colors of each chakra and the energy frequency of each color needed for optimal health of mind, body and spirit. The sun enters through the top of the head and retinas of the eyes traveling through the top of your brain fusing it with energy, then down your spinal cord energizing all of your chakras and organs. Earthing is also an essential part of connecting with universal source energy. Walking barefoot on the grass or a walk on the beach are simple ways to ground. Sometimes I'll sit in my yard and ground while I read. You can also find indoor grounding mats online great for colder climates or rainy days. Many athletes use these mats to maintain optimal balanced energy. Earth has enough energy to light up this whole planet... but that's a whole story in itself.

Binary beats are also very beneficial in keeping the brain and energy centers spiritually tuned in so to speak. A few I found to be beneficial are, Holosync, Solfeggio and Kelly Howell. These brain wave sound frequencies work to synchronize the right and left hemispheres of the brain. This has all helped me land so to speak, and stay tuned into the now. The present time awareness, instead of worrying about what happened yesterday or what's going on next week. This also helps slow down the traffic jam of thoughts in our busy overloaded minds; it's a fast paced world we now live in. Now as a static free grounded clear channel, I am better able to receive spiritual guidance. I really get and understand on a deeper level now the true meaning of "The body is the Temple of God."

CHAPTER 10

AS ABOVE SO BELOW

Alchemy was said to have originated in Egypt where Thoth is thought to be the original author of science, medicine, mathematics, geometry, philosophy, and the codes of the stars and heavens, in other words matter. His feminine counterpart Ma`at was known as the force that maintained the universe, the spirit. Thoth and Ma`at brought the elements together, the two becoming one still known today as "Hermes Trismegistus" This was the birth of the Hermetic tradition known as Alchemy. When the ancient Hermetic practice of Alchemy was coveted by dark secret societies and used for dark purposes, in my opinion this was one of the worst deceptions and tragedies of our existence.

One of the foundational manuscripts of Alchemy is "The Emerald Tablet" believed to contain the secrets of the art. One of the most common translations was done by Isaac Newton who from translation wrote: "Tis true without lying, certain and most true. That which is below, is like that which is above to do the miracles of one only thing. As all things have been and arose from one by the meditation of one" Below are the seven corresponding Hermetic principals of Alchemy.

The Seven Hermetic Principals

I. MENTALISM

The all is mind, the Universe is mental

The crown chakra and the pituitary gland

The first glad to appear in the Human Embryo

II. CORRESPONDENCE

As above so below as below so above

The Brow Chakra and the Pineal Gland

The Pineal gland produces the "Melatonin"

that controls the waking and sleeping cycles.

III. VIBRATION

Nothing rests everything moves everything vibrates

The throat chakra and the thyroid gland

The thyroid gland produces "Thyroxin" to convert

oxygen and food into usable energy

IV. POLARITY

Everything is dual, has poles, and has its pair of opposites. Like and unlike are the same opposites, they are identical in nature, but different in degree, all truths are but half-truths all paradoxes may be reconciled.

The heart chakra and the thymus gland

The thymus gland produces "T cells" for the immune system of the body.

V. RHYTHM (The Cycles)

Everything flows out and in, everything has its tides. All things rise and fall, the pendulum-swing manifests in everything. The measure of the swing to the right is the measure of the swing to the left, rhythm compensates.

The naval chakra and the adrenal gland

The adrenal gland produces the "Hydrocortisone" that regulates the use of food and helps the body adjust to stress.

VI. CAUSE AND EFFECT

Every cause has its effect; every effect has its cause. Everything happens according to law, chance is but a name for law not recognized. There are many planes of causation, but nothing escapes the law.

The spleen chakra and the spleen

The Spleen produces "Macrophages" to cleanse the blood and is vital to the immune system of the body and a person's health.

VII. GENDER

Gender is in everything, everything has its masculine and feminine principles, gender manifests on all planes.

The root chakra, the sacral or reproductive glands

The reproductive organs of "male and female" in all Life forms that exist.

Alchemy is an advanced spiritual discipline. The true Alchemist wasn't trying to turn lead into gold although the casual observer may think so from how things were presented. Rather they were striving to turn the lead of an undeveloped consciousness into the gold of a fully realized and enlightened soul. You are a divine being; you come from divine light and to divine light you will return. Now is the time we are awakening to our universal calling, under the credo of the Emerald Tablet.

CHAPTER 11

BEINGS OF LIGHT

All of creation whether we believe it or not doesn't just revolve around us. Hate to break it to yah but God has created many other beings along with us to serve in creation and co-creation. In fact unless you live under a rock you're aware of sightings and encounters with several beings especially over the last decade. These sightings are about to increase dramatically to prepare us for the mass arrival and landings that are emanate for them to better assist us. A state of denial seems to be comfortable for most people when it comes to anything misunderstood. It's really sad when you stop to think about it, especially since they are full of pure love and light. The fact is these beings of light were created by God to serve God and are now as we speak assisting our creator and source of all life, to keep us from total destruction of ourselves and our planet. These beings of light are not going away, so embrace the fact and prepare for a complete disclosure of why the government has tried so hard to suppress the truth in the first place. Creating outright lies and fear propaganda through media and recent movie releases of alien destruction of planet earth.

It's no coincidence; these seeds are planted in the minds of the masses to create fear when they do arrive. Give me a break don't you think they seem to be a little more advanced than us! Got some good news for you, extraterrestrials are here to help free us from the tyranny of the dark cabals group of puppet masters behind the curtain generating the next campaign of fear to serve the dark agenda of the Illuminati. The dark cabal's agenda never serves the best interest of humanity; they want you to fund the next world war. Illuminati and all other secret societies of the dark cabal know the Federation of Light and the Ascended Masters are here to remove them from power once and for all. Heaven has heard the cries of the children dying in our war ravaged streets of the mothers who can't feed their own babies, of the homeless, jobless, joyless souls that can't figure out what life's about anymore. The once hopeful are now feeling hopeless. Together we can all rise above the oppression and assist in the co-creation of the Golden Age; we are the generation that has been prophesied about. Slow down long enough in your busy day to see the beauty that surrounds you, the smile of a child, the sweet scent of flowers, the majesty of earth and all its inhabitants. Let's stop focusing on what's not working and build from what is working; it's time for real change not more broken promises. What we collectively focus on expands this isn't some hocus pocus saying, it's a scientific fact of cause and effect, metaphysics and the law of attraction. If you can think it you can achieve it, ask and you shall receive, knock and it shall be opened unto you. When did we start feeling so small, helpless, and insignificant? We are the direct descendants of God Almighty our Creator the Alpha and the Omega it is our birthright to be prosperous, joyous, and free to co-create and co-habitat earth as one. How did we allow all the separatism, judgment, violence, and loss of our own power to escalate to the point of needing other beings to have to come help us fix anything? We should be ashamed, but that won't fix anything. Gratitude, love and appreciation would be a great start, we need to do everything possible to assist in helping clean up the mess we are all part of creating. I have been blessed to have traveled to so many beautiful places and experience the true beauty of our planet. We have been fed so much deception that most people don't know what's real anymore. The truth is we have been working for the real terrorist for centuries and we are about to be freed from slavery and ushered into a new paradigm, a new reality, pay attention and you'll see the signs of the times everywhere. Not just here on earth but even the signs from beyond our immediate realm. We only have to pay attention to the signs and open our hearts and our minds to the guidance that is available to all who seek the answers. We are all one from one source; we can no longer allow race, creed, religion or lack of, to separate us.

We have to stop talking about the change we want to see and experience, and actually stand up and be accountable by contributing to it. Mother Earth has sustained us generation after generation and now she needs all of us to help her heal. We are the generation that has had enough; we can no longer be part of the problem. We are forging ahead with the solutions, we are strong and we are many. We will no longer play by the old rules we are making new rules now that will make this game of life fun for all to play. Come play with us we are all one, from one source.

For more information on how to be part of this great shift of humanity and some resources to help assist you on your journey visit my website at www. KundaliniQuest.com I can only hope that in sharing my story I have helped someone else on this journey, I feel as though my life has just begun. I truly feel a new freedom and happiness, unlike anything I've ever felt before. If I can help another human being along the way then my life has taken on a deeper more meaningful purpose. The heart is more powerful than the mind, if only we could all exercise heart based thinking rather than ego based thinking we could easily change the world in which we live.

EPILOGUE

Now let's do an overview, I want to shed a little light on each area so we can connect the dots and get ourselves reunified and energized. Try to keep an open mind at all times during this section of the book. We have to go back now to Thoth and Ma`at and the deception of the dark cabal, known today as the illuminati and Freemasons. This was one of the main suppressions of knowledge weakening our connection to Mother Earth and Father God and the unified field of consciousness. Knowledge is power only if you possess it. This is when things got really twisted and this occult began. First, let's look at what occult means because for most it means the practice of dark magic. All occult means is hidden, a secret, something kept in the dark. For the sake of understanding the depth of this hidden secret we need to know this so we can remove the negative energy from this simple word. The dark cabal from this point in ancient history to this very moment in time has spent all of its waking hours and energy to harness ours. These societies practice and covet the Art of Alchemy protected by an oath of death to anyone that reveals its secrets. This is when the deception of the church was introduced and power and control of the masses became the goal.

You see, as I said knowledge is power therefore whomever possess the knowledge possess the power. Today you will possess some of this knowledge and with it the power to choose to better connect to our Creator and the Universe. Alchemy as practiced by Jesus and the Essenes teaches us as children of God how to stay energetically connected. We are like a light switch when it's off the power is still connected but you have to turn the switch on to receive the light. The dark cabal knew this so while they were practicing the power of Alchemy and coveting it, the rest of humanity were becoming lost and detached from source. This is when the deception of the church began, anyone outside of these societies caught practicing the art of Alchemy were stoned, burned, flogged, and imprisoned for witchcraft or blasphemy. We are still detached and they are presently very strongly united.

Throughout time we have been a big part of our own disconnection and separation from source at will without a realization of what's going on around us. So let's fast forward to our current situation to better understand some of the keywords I gave you earlier. For those of you who may not have done a little research in the area of HAARP or Chemtrails it's important to have an understanding of them at this point.

HAARP was created by the dark cabal to interfere with the torus surrounding our planet, when this magnetic field is manipulated in any way it causes static that affects our whole ionosphere. Most importantly to note here is it also affects our body's energetic spiritual connection to our divine source. This torus generates its energy from the magnetic polarity pull of earth and the sun. This same torus of energy runs along our spine and through each of our chakras and around us at a certain speed and frequency. HAARP causes interference in this vital energy field that surrounds our body.

We need to take a closer look at Chemtrails at this point to better understand the affects it has on us. The main culprit in this chemical cocktail of poisons is aluminum; this has been sprayed via aircraft on mankind for years, hence all the trails instead of billowing beautiful clouds. Along with the many arrests as mentioned earlier, chemtrail planes are being seized.

So soon expect to see more of the clouds many of our children have never even seen. Now back to the subject, some of the many affects aluminum has on our energetic body and our planet. Aluminum toxicity causes Alzheimer's disease, hyperparathyroidism, anemia, kidney dysfunction, liver dysfunction, colitis, neuromuscular disorders, dental cavities, Parkinson's disease, dementia, ulcers etc. aluminum shorts out our circuits and poisons our minds our bodies our water and top soil affecting our whole eco system. The Illuminati along with their culprit secret societies spend all of their waking moments finding ways to keep us dying and dulled down to a controllable level, through the polar opposite of what we need to stay energetically connected, mentally fit and spiritually strong. So let's talk about salt now, real holistic salt not poisonous refined table salt. Himalayan salt or any holistic salts are infused with essential minerals needed in our blood for our thyroid to function the way it's intended to function. Table salt actually poisons the thyroid, most importantly to understand here once again is this cuts off the energy needed for the chakra associated with the thyroid. Once this chakra is shut down or wacked out we cannot attain the heightened spiritual connection or enlightenment we are created to experience. It's as though the light was switched off, we know the power is on and we can intuitively feel it, but just can't seem to get to that spiritual place we know exists.

Now let's shed some light on symbolism I want to take a moment to first say most symbols of dark were originally symbols of light that were altered, I am going to use the caduceus for an example. This symbolism anciently known in Alchemy is signified by the rising of the winged serpent dragons toward enlightenment. This Kundalini awakening ignites the base or first chakra located at the base of the spine represented by the color red. Once awakened the journey toward enlightenment begins to manifest in a fierce and powerful spiral of source energy up the spine awakening all seven chakras and your DNA code. The dark cabal in knowing this altered the original symbol of enlightenment by removing the wings of the Dragon to signify an inability to ever achieve true enlightenment and placed the wings from the dragon above the dragons now depicted as lowly serpents trapped below the wings they once possessed.

As far as Kundalini rising is concerned it is the masculine and feminine aspects of every human being becoming one and ascending to enlightenment. We are changing and evolving in fact human DNA is changing that is why so many people have been experiencing body aches, blurred vision, and headaches to name a few symptoms its all part of our evolution. Chances are high that your DNA is being activated and your chakras need a tune up so to speak. In fact, you are like a car that's been parked for so long the gas evaporated and it needs some fuel to get started not to mention the battery needs a good charge. Once you get it running then you can clean up the inside and get the radio tuned in so the static is gone and you can hear the music again. So let's do that, we don't have to do it overnight, let's just get some fuel and charge the battery. The fuel is what we eat and drink; this will be different for everyone, so let's just introduce a few things into your routine and start simple, then allow your own intuition to start guiding you. Let's start with simply changing our salt; our body needs salt. We just need the right kind of salt, holistic salt, I use pink Himalayan salt. This is easy to find as more and more people are waking up and realizing what's going on. Let's try to introduce some organic live fruits and vegetables into your meals; raw not cooked. It is a fact that one organic apple has more energy than the three average cooked nutritionally dead meals consumed throughout the course of a day.

We also need to drink plenty of water throughout the day not all water is created equal; some waters are processed and altered making them full of chemicals and chlorine. Most of what is missing from all the processing is what our bodies truly need. We need the silica and minerals that can only be found in water bottled at the source real artesian holistic water. Because I live in the city I use Fiji and know that it has what my body needs and it's easy to find. Next, whenever possible get those shoes off and allow the energy from the earth into your chakra system, this will keep your battery charged. A walk in the park on the beach; whatever works for you. Whatever works for you. As I shared with you earlier athletes now understand the importance of being grounded. I also hope you really get the importance of the seven rays of light that emit from the sun in sound frequency and color. The seven colors of the rainbow are the same colors in our chakra or chi center these energetic frequencies are another vital missing link better connecting us to our divine source that's been broken. These rays of light enter the retina, travel through the brain center and down the spine through our chakras and out through our feet back into earth. Keeping us aligned with the grid, we are all part of the mind of God. Breathing is also vital for healthy brain function, just breathe deeply in through your nose and out through your mouth.

You don't have to be a yogi or some guru to breathe deeply with intention, attention and gratitude throughout your day. It just helps keep you grounded and sends oxygen to your brain releasing melatonin and that alone will lower anyone's stress level. Once your grounded you'll intuitively want to meditate and learn more about who you really are, it is then that the answers will come. Ask and you shall receive, knock and the door shall be opened. This is an amazing time to be alive my friend, so lets wake up. Walking around half-awake with no real energy for life or love is not going to work in 2012 and beyond, 2012 is the year of power. This is also the year of the water dragon, symbolizing happiness and great prosperity, this only occurs once every twelve years. You will be amazed at what a little holistic salt, water, sun, raw food and earthing will do for you. It is my intention that this book somehow helps to inspire you and that at the least a seed has been planted that will be watered along the way. Enjoy your journey into the Promised Land.

ACKNOWLEDGMENTS

To my Partner Amanda her son Andrew and daughter Crystal for the unconditional love and enduring support through my constant need of quiet space to study, research, read and write. Feeling accepted and loved through my countless sleepless nights. And all of the pains, emotions, confusion and changes in sleeping and eating patterns associated with the awakening. We have all learned so much as a family on this amazing spiritual journey. I am truly blessed and grateful to have them in my life.

To Voloque the collective consciousness of 11 White Winged Angels for constant guidance and continued support. The calming energy waves of love, and peace when I need it most, all the signs that continue to light a clear path for me, to see, hear and intuitively know what to do next. For this gift and all that I have learned and continue to learn about the true nature of our Creator, the Universe and our place in it. I am truly grateful and blessed.

"In Loving Memory of my Grandmother Marjorie"

My Dear Ones

Always remember my dear ones. That kind words and a tender smile will bring happiness to a lonely one. You will feel happy and gay knowing you did your bit that day.

Always remember my dear ones. When the darkest cloud surrounds you and in despair you see no way, always remember the light of faith, it will always lead the way.

Always remember dear ones. Happiness doesn't come with riches, nor to be a king on a throne. A kind thought and a forgiving heart will always find a way.

By Marjorie Lewis